Read • Think • Do

MATH

Ages 5 & Up

Measuring
Book 2

Ann Montague-Smith

Teacher Created Resources

Copyright © QEB Publishing 2004

First published in the United States by
QEB Publishing, Inc.
23062 La Cadena Drive
Laguna Hills
CA 92653

This edition published by
Teacher Created Resources, Inc.
6421 Industry Way
Westminster, CA 92683

www.teachercreated.com

Library of Congress Control Number: 2004102089

ISBN 1-4206-8171-0

Written by Ann Montague-Smith
Designed and edited by The Complete Works
Illustrated by Jenny Tulip
Photography by Steve Lumb and Michael Wicks

Creative Director Louise Morley
Editorial Manager Jean Coppendale

Printed and bound in China

With thanks to:

Contents

Comparing lengths

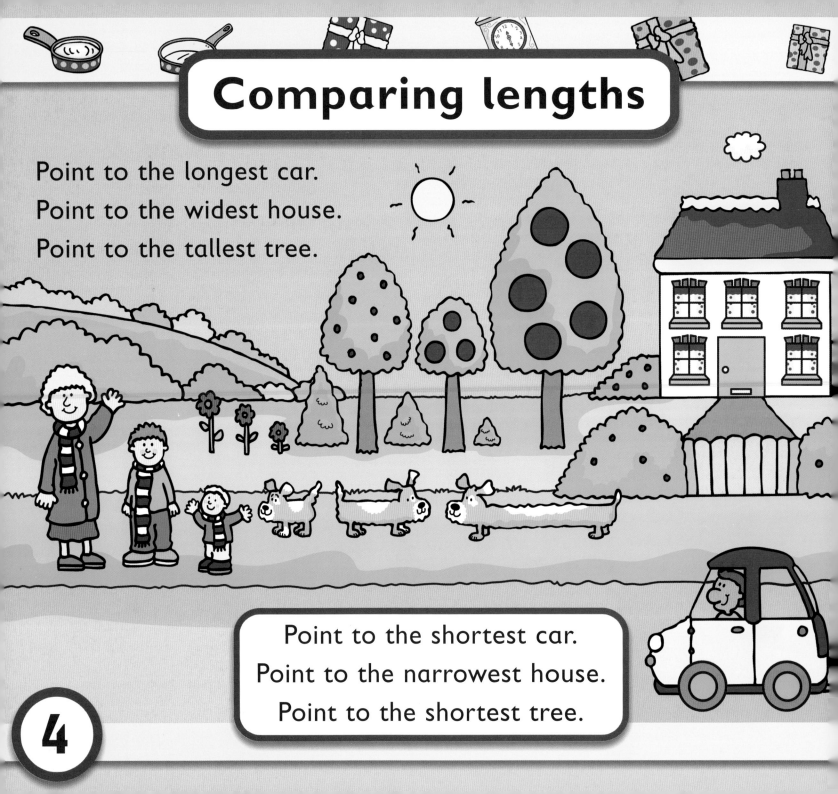

Point to the longest car.
Point to the widest house.
Point to the tallest tree.

Point to the shortest car.
Point to the narrowest house.
Point to the shortest tree.

Challenge

Choose 4 toys. Put them in order. Start with the narrowest. Now do this again. Start with the shortest. Is the order the same? Why do you think that is?

Measuring lengths

Put a strip of paper along one of the cats. Cut the strip so that it is just as long as the cat. Now put the strip along the mouse ruler. How long is the cat? Measure to find the longest cat.

Which cat is the shortest?

Challenge

Use the mouse ruler to help you find toys which are about 4 mice long. Find toys which you think are shorter than 4 mice. Check with the mouse ruler.

Heaviest and lightest

Look at each balance.
Which package is heavier?
Which package is lighter?

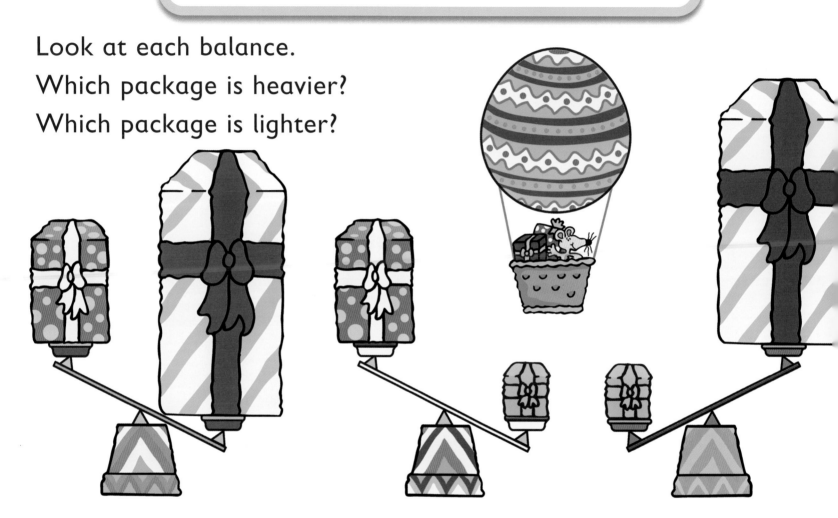

Look at the three balances again. Can you figure out which package is heaviest? Which is lightest?

Challenge

Get some play dough.
Make 3 packages.
Guess the order
of the packages.
Start with the lightest.
Now use a balance
to check.

9

How much does it hold?

Look at the pairs of containers.

Will all the water from the full container fit into the empty one?

Look at the green cup, teapot, and bowl.

Which do you think will hold more than the bowl?

Which do you think will hold less than the bowl?

Challenge

Find 3 bottles of different sizes.
Decide which you think holds
the least and which holds the most.
Check by filling and pouring.
Did you make a good guess?

Which bucket do you think will hold the most sand?

Which shovel do you think will hold the most sand?

Challenge

Put 4 glasses that are the same size in a line. Leave the first glass empty and fill the last one to the top with water. How much water will you need to pour into the others so they are in order from least to most?

Sequencing

Look at the pictures.

Which picture starts the story?

Tell the story in the correct order.

Down came the rain
And washed the spider out;

So the Itsy Bitsy Spider
Climbed up the spout again.

Say the rhyme and point to the pictures in order.

Challenge

What did you do today? Tell a friend what you did today. Start with getting up this morning.

Itsy Bitsy Spider
Climbed up the water spout;

Out came the sun
And dried up all the rain;

Days of the week

What does Sam do on Sunday?
What does Sam do on the other days of the week?

On Sunday, Sam visited his grandparents.

On Monday, Sam went to school.

On Tuesday, Sam we
swimming with his do

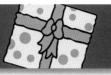

Wednesday, Sam ate
ghetti and meatballs.

Challenge

What do you do each day
of the week? Draw a
picture for each
day of the week.

On Thursday, Sam
elped wash the car.

On Friday, Sam
went shopping.

On Saturday, Sam
played in the park.

O'clock

What time is it?

Which clock shows 5 o'clock?

Can you say all the clock times?

18

Challenge

You will need a clock. You say an o'clock time to a friend. Ask your friend to show this time on the clock.

19

I know about the words...

Get some board-game tokens.

Listen to each word.

Put a token on the picture that matches the words.

8 o'clock

4 o'clock

widest

narrowest

longest

shortest

tallest   **shortest**

Challenge

Find some containers. Which one is the tallest? Which holds the most? Which is the shortest? Which holds the least?

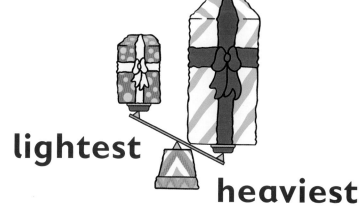

lightest   **heaviest**

holds most   **holds more**   **holds less**   **holds least**

21

Supporting notes for adults

Comparing lengths – pages 4-5

Discuss the size order of each set, such as, "Which is the shortest tree? So which tree comes next?" Use the other sets of 3 objects in the picture in the same way.

Measuring lengths – pages 6-7

Show the children how to use the mouse ruler. Encourage the children to count the mice to find out how long each cat is.

Heaviest and lightest – pages 8-9

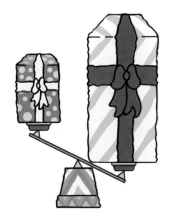

Begin by comparing the packages on each balance. Now ask the children to decide which must be the heaviest of all and to say why they think that.

How much does it hold? – pages 10-11

Encourage the children to explain which pan they think will hold more/less. Check that they can use the vocabulary of "full," "empty," "holds more/less…"

Most and least – pages 12-13

The children are likely to have different views about which bucket or shovel holds the most. This activity is designed to encourage a lot of talking about how much they think each one will hold, so ask the children to compare the buckets and explain their thinking.

Sequencing – pages 14-15

If the children do not know the rhyme, say it for them and ask them to point to the relevant picture each time.

Days of the week – pages 16-17

Say the days of the week together in order. Ask questions such as, "What day is it today? What day was it yesterday? What day will it be tomorrow? What days do you go to school?"

O'clock – pages 18-19

If the children are unsure about telling time, provide some clock faces and ask them to set their clocks to the times on the page.

I know about the words… – pages 20-21

Read the words under each picture. Ask the children to say which picture shows that word. Some of the picture will have 2 ideas, such as heaviest and lightest. Encourage the children to show you which part of the picture depicts each idea.

Suggestions for using this book

Children will enjoy looking through the book and talking about the colorful pictures. Sit somewhere comfortable together. Read the instructions to the children, then encourage them to take part in the activity and check whether or not they understand what to do.

The activities encourage children to compare three things for length, weight or capacity. Ask the children to decide the order of the three things, such as for length, by putting them in order from shortest to longest. Always encourage them to guess first, so that they are making an estimate. Then they can make comparisons to check if they made a good guess. Estimating skills improve with practice and through checking by measuring.

In capacity, where children are filling and pouring from containers, they may need to be reminded that in everyday life we do not fill things to the brim. Encourage them to talk about what would happen if we tried to drink from a cup that was full to the brim. However, when filling and pouring, and especially when using dry sand, children will want to fill containers up to the brim.

Children are introduced to the concept of time in this book. Encourage them to talk about things that they have done, and to put the events into order. This will help them to sequence events and to understand that something happens first, then the next thing happens… and so on. Ask questions about the days of the week, such as "What day is it today? What day will it be tomorrow… What was it yesterday?" Children will begin to recognize times on the clock. Help them to link the time shown on the clock to everyday events, such as what time they get up.